The Rules Of Successful Entrepreneurs

Learn The Rules, Change The Game, Be The Winner

Peter Jason Clarke

New project

The Rules Of Successful Entrepreneurs

Please note the information contained within this document is for educational and entertainment purposes only. All effort has been executed to present accurate, up to date, and reliable, complete information. No warranties of any kind are declared or implied. Readers acknowledge that the author is not engaging in the rendering of legal, financial, medical or professional advice. The content within this book has been derived from various sources. Please consult a licensed professional before attempting any techniques outlined in this book.

By reading this document, the reader agrees that under no circumstances is the author responsible for any losses, direct or indirect, which are incurred as a result of the use of information contained within this document, including, but not limited to, — errors, omissions, or inaccuracies.

Table Of Contents

The Rules Of Successful Entrepreneurs

Chapter 1: Foundation in Financial IQ

Definition Of Insanity

Naturally, most if not all of us want and crave for something better. It is all part of us if we want a bigger car, a better house, buying good things for the family. We keep hoping for more but, in order to get what you don't have, you have got to do something you have never done before.

That simply means:

Doing the <u>same</u> thing over and over again YET expecting <u>different</u> results!

The Rules Of Successful Entrepreneurs

As an employee, you can't stay at the same job forever and hope that a miracle will happen and your boss will suddenly give you a raise. You will be lucky that there is no downsizing in your company. Switching to another company will only provide a short term solution to a long term problem.

Sure, you can take up a second or even third job, but do you have enough hours and stamina in a day to sustain it?

<u>The bottom-line</u>: Trading time for money isn't wise financial sense in the long term. You keep on increasing the hours just to win the rat race, but in the end of the day, you are still a rat on the mill!

Increasing your wages only puts you in a higher tax bracket. Your salaries increase but so does your expenses on your house and car. How will you invest in yourself when all the time you spend working for a company, working for the government paying taxes and working for the bank paying off your house and car? What if you fall sick and can't work tomorrow? Will the government take care of your family?

I highly doubt so.

So isn't it time you take your finances a tad more seriously?

What Is Money?

You see, there are many ideas of what people think money is.

Some say it is a form of measurement.

Yes, but a measurement of what? Wealth? In the olden days, people measured wealth by how many cows, sheep and horses they had. But do people measure wealth today by your cows and horses? How about slaves? Was there a time where manpower is considered a hot commodity? Are slaves worth anything today? Are your dollar bills sitting in the bank going to protect you if a recession strikes the country? No, wealth can not be measured by the dollar bill.

Some say it is a form of power.

Yes, money can give you power, but if you are stuck on a desert island forever with a trillion dollars, will that money mean squat to you? If someone offered you water and a helicopter to fly out of there, you would trade all your money in a split second, so money is not an accurate measurement of power – it heavily depends on how and wisely you use it (*hint!*).

Many believe *it is the root of all evil...* and several others take on this belief without much questioning.

Now, now, now... money is **NOT** the root of all evil (*otherwise, why do you think churches still accept monetary donation and charity?*). **The love of money** is the root of all evil. Remember, money is an excellent servant but a terrible master. If you are trading your life away for the dollar, money then has power over your time and life.

And unless you have proper financial intelligence, the lack of money can spawn a lot of evil thinking and negative mindset as observed in primarily cheats, thieves, criminals, breakups, freeloaders, cheapskates, and more to name.

But what is money, really?

Money is an idea, backed by confidence.

While money has naturally been developed by merchants in the older days to replace the questionable barter system, money today is literally invented by the rich and wealthy.

Entrepreneurs are willing to part with their money to buy other people's time. Other people's time i.e. *employees and self-employed people* becomes their employer's asset and the employers this priceless resource to go on to create more wealth for themselves.

And here's the thing: **as long as you work for money, you are enslaved by it! 80% - 90%** of the populations today are being *enslaved* involuntarily.

What we don't realize is that there is a part of our soul that cannot be bought at whatever price. Would you chop off your little finger if your boss offered you 24 months of your salary immediately? You and I know we are worth more than that. But when you hear of cases of people selling their body parts for cash in some countries, we can have our eyeballs pop out of our eye sockets.

On the other hand, we occasionally DO sell out a part of ourselves for money like a donkey and a carrot.

Awareness Before Change

Now **don't get me wrong**: I'm not banging on working at a job (I worked at one before I became an Internet Entrepreneur).

But let's face it: our needs today are growing more than ever before in any period of history. Prices go up, salaries don't. There are more baby boomers than ever and have very little pension to show for their decades of years of work efforts.

And there is no guessing to how many people really, really hate the unhealthy, hectic lifestyle of getting up early, coping with stress for most parts of the day, join traffic jams, spend more money and time in traveling, enjoy very little rest, and <u>repeat</u> the viscous cycle.

Definitely doesn't paint a nice financial and lifestyle picture, huh?

The Rules Of Successful Entrepreneurs

The first step to change is to **be aware of the problem**. <u>Awareness before change</u> (or ABC for short) is necessary if you are to make any changes in life to start taking control of your financial life and then get out of the rat race.

We need the awareness to know what state we are in so we know where we are going. For starters, indulge me in a quick exercise as we exit this chapter shortly:

Time And Money

There are generally 4 types of people in the world:

(1) **No time, and no money.**

Most employees fall into the category. You can't go shopping on a Tuesday afternoon or fire your boss whenever you like. Most employees can't even save money in their pension to last 3 years!

(2) **No time, lots of money.**

Self-employed, professionals and small business owners are in this category. They are slightly better off than the employee because they earn more, but they have to work even harder than employees to keep up with the diminishing profit margins, competition and servicing their customers.

(3) **Got time, no money.**

A lot of farmers, villagers, college dropouts or bums have lots of time but no money. Maybe ignorance is bliss, but without a stable source of income, how long can you last many days forward?

(4) **Got time, and lots of money.**

It is the category that big business owners, landlords, investors are in. Imagine, not having to work for money, but having money to work for you by investing them and earning profits by using your money to make money.

Short Quiz

1. Which one of the four categories are you currently in?

1. Which one category do you desire to be in tomorrow?

Chapter 2: Ways To Achieve Wealth

2 Wealth Building Models

Everyone wants to make more money, but people are generally split into two categories:

Those who bring results after they are promised wealth first

Or

Those who bring the results first, then are rewarded by others afterwards

Let's explore the two groups in depth.

Those who only move their butts after promised big fat paychecks are more like employees, freshmen, or mercenaries.

The Rules Of Successful Entrepreneurs

There is no right or no wrong with this kind of thinking, but consider: you are once again, trading your precious time for money. Instead of investing your time in an ASSET that generates money, you spend your time working on something that is short term, limited wealth, and does not give you income long after you have stopped working.

Consider also, that this kind of short term vision will only produce limited or temporary results at best. Ever seen a security guard asleep at work when the boss is not around?

Furthermore, the part where our emotions get the better of us is when we allow our lives to be run by chasing the dollar. It is evident whenever an employee is offered a higher salary, more medical benefits and longer vacations, that their heart starts pumping faster.

The Rules Of Successful Entrepreneurs

A higher salary doesn't mean less financial problems. On the contrary when your income goes up, your commitments, your tax bracket and your time spent in your company increases. **The greater your salary, the weaker your position** because if your boss is paying you a 5 figure income and calls for an emergency meeting, *you had better rush over to the office even if you are halfway making love to your wife!*

I think the best definition of an employee/boss relationship can be summed up as this.

An employee will only do the bare minimum to keep the boss from firing them and a boss will only pay the bare minimum to keep an employee from leaving.

Now let's explore the other group.

There are many creative people, inventors, entrepreneurs, and business leaders who fall into this category.

An entrepreneur is someone who always has good ideas.

The Rules Of Successful Entrepreneurs

The first obstacle we need to overcome if we want to succeed in the second group is to **stop working for money**. What does this mean? Isn't making money part and parcel of having good financial IQ?

What I mean by 'stop working for money' is not working for free. Rather, it means work so as to gain the necessary skills you need to be a successful entrepreneur (or inventor, investor). Allow me to illustrate:

If you lack the contacts for running a business, where would the best place be to look for contacts? Of course, your competitor's customers.

How about product knowledge? Then work with a company that will teach you all the ins and outs of the tricks of the trade.

Not familiar with the production line of a factory? Work in one! Learn the ropes or manage the factory workers.

Fear of talking to people? Get a sales job where you will be forced to talk to lots of people. It is also a great way to develop perseverance!

The Rules Of Successful Entrepreneurs

Don't you know that the best education you can get is in real life! Not at a lecture hall.

The bottom-line is: **not everybody has what it takes to succeed as an entrepreneur!**

It is not that easy. Many lack the perseverance, the creative mindset, the financial capabilities or the necessary people to get the job done and usually give up too early before any results can be seen! The fastest way to get those skills to succeed is to learn them hands on and you even get paid in the process! Don't get absorbed with how much you are paid.

When Donald Trump was selecting candidates in *The Apprentice*, their first task was to go to the streets and sell lemonade! Many would find it a degrading task. But to The Donald, it was very important: If you can't even do something as simple as sell lemonade, how on earth can you handle a daunting task like running the Trump Empire?

Again, let me emphasize:

Would you trade time for short term money? (Money stops coming in when you stop)

Or

Trade time and money for a long term asset that generates you income? (Even long after you have stopped)

God created us with a brain. All we need to do is look around us and observe problems to overcome because every problem is an opportunity in disguise.

It is all up to you. You may or may not see the results in the short term, but by using our brains and the resources around us, we can create true value that others are willing to pay for what we have to offer.

3 Ways of Making Money

Let me summarize the 3 Ways of Making Money

Trading Time For Money - employees, self-employed

Manifesting & Using Creative Ideas - inventors, artists, programmers

Leveraging on resources and other people - business people, leaders

The Rules Of Successful Entrepreneurs

If you are a professional, have you ever explored writing an e-book about your field of expertise? If well written, it could provide a new income stream, instead of you selling out your time serving your clients.

How about a computer programmer? You can come out with your own revolutionary product instead of selling your ideas to the company you work for.

How about real estate, instead of selling houses, you can pool financial sources to buy houses cheap, increase their value and sell them off at a higher price. It just takes a little time and research to find good ideas.

Is money a problem? Seek out loans if you can take the risk. Pool money from many investors or seek a grant. The sky is the limit when it comes to making money.

Again, which way do you want to achieve wealth? Answer: it's totally up to you

Chapter 3: The Most Important Rule in Investing

What Does Investing Mean To People?

What comes in to your mind when you mention the word investing?

Does it mean, putting your money in insurance, mutual funds, the stock market or even high-yield investments?

Other people might only think about investing when they are about to die and they haven't left anything for their offspring.

Some even shiver when they hear the word, often claiming that they have no money to invest or feel that is too complicated a subject to even discuss about.

Many people even invest heavily in health supplements, personal trainers and beauticians to make themselves live longer, healthier or even look younger! Imagine the advertising budget for beauty companies nowadays.

All these are legitimate concerns when it comes to investing, but I am talking about the most important investment a person can make in his lifetime.

Invest in Yourself

The most important and No.1 rule is "Invest in Yourself" – if you don't, who else will?

Your parents will only invest in your education only until you leave college. But that is just the basic necessities provided and does not teach you important lessons about financial education.

Would you depend on colleges or universities to teach you how to make money? Most colleges only teach you skills so you can earn money working for other people. How about business school? Honestly, if business lecturers are such experts at business, why are they still lecturing there instead of making a fortune in business ventures?

The Rules Of Successful Entrepreneurs

Would your boss teach you how to succeed in business so that one day, you will be in his position?

You and only you have to be proactive enough to take that responsibility

You see, when you invest in yourself, it means taking on the importance of educating yourself. Education not in the academic or technical sense, though they are necessary skills to be developed in life. Our education doesn't stop at college.

For most working adults, their education enters retardation stage after they leave college. They stop learning and therefore they stop growing. They only grow sideways from eating too much pizzas or take-out during their busy lunch breaks.

The Rules Of Successful Entrepreneurs

We know that IQ is important right? But why aren't the most intelligent people in the world the richest people in the world? There are many accountants and financial planners rushing to their cars every evening trying to beat the after work traffic congestions! They are not rich!

How about EQ or Emotional quotient? Do working hard, having a great attitude and a positive mindset solve our financial situation? These are important when running a business, but let me illustrate:

If you are driving from Boston to New York using the wrong road map, you won't get to our destination no matter how fast you drive your car (working hard)! You can work harder, but you would only get to the wrong destination faster! You may have the best attitude in the world or the most positive mindset, but you still won't get to New York (although the journey wouldn't bother you since you are feeling positive about it)

The Importance Of Financial Education

You must FIRST invest in your Financial IQ.

The Rules Of Successful Entrepreneurs

Having good financial IQ is not about saving tons of money or dumping them into mutual funds. It is developing a healthy relationship money and building a wealth of assets that will generate you money.

What does it take to develop your financial IQ?

Delayed gratification is one of the most important aspects to developing your financial IQ. Take this as a hypothetical example.

Would you pay for a pint of milk or a cow?

If you buy milk, it is consumed and it is over. You will have to buy milk over and over again when it is finished. Even if the milk costs less than a cow, in the long run, you will still be buying milk again and again.

Now, if a cow were to cost 50 times more than milk, you might pay through your nose when you purchase the cow, but after consuming 50 pints worth of milk from the cow, you would break even on your investment and save more money in the future. In fact, the cow might give birth to 2 or more calves and you could sell one of them for profit!

Get the idea?

The Rules Of Successful Entrepreneurs

EVERYONE is capable of **creating wealth.** When you take a beat up old car and give it an overhaul, paint it with a new coat of paint, and change a few more parts to make it start running again, you could sell that car for more money than if it was just a beat up old car. You would have created wealth in the process!

How about a farm? If you turn a farm into a country home getaway resort, wouldn't the value of the farm land increase manifold?

It is the same principle for chefs, computer programmers and craftsmen. The sum of the whole is greater than the parts. We are all capable of creating wealth even out of thin air and that is the first step to getting our creative juices flowing.

The value of anything is defined by **supply and demand**.

You don't need to be a Major in economics to understand this. Money is just an idea. Remember the desert island example? The true measurement of money is not the cents or dollars it represents.

If you have developed a product that people want, would they pay more to you than usual? Would you apply your skills in creating good assets?

<u>Bottom-line</u> is this:

Invest in assets that bring long term value. Anything that brings you more income is an asset. Don't invest too much in liabilities like cars or boats.

Even houses are not considered assets until they are fully paid off (If you lost your job tomorrow and you can't pay for your house, is your house an asset or liability?)

Are you willing to step out of your comfort zone and pay the price for financial IQ or ignore the signs of the times and expect your boss, the government and the bank to take care of you financially for the rest of your life, living below your means and never taking risks to better your family's future?

Chapter 4: Why Do So Many Internet Startups Fail Today?

Everyday out there in the real brick and mortar world, millions and millions of people drag themselves from the warm, warm beds, take a shower, grab a cup of coffee, and head off to their jobs as they are thinking that there has got to be an easier way to make a living.

Every one of those millions and millions of people knows somebody who has quit the 'get-up-and-go-to-work' grind and is making a very good living by working on their personal computers from the comfort of their own homes.

Working from home sounds like an ideal solution to them. Many of these dissatisfied souls will quit their jobs and plunge head-first into internet marketing with no preparation, no knowledge of what they are doing, no education, and no hope of success. Failure is their only option and they don't even suspect.

The Rules Of Successful Entrepreneurs

The fact is that according to many sources, more than 90% (Ninety percent) of all Internet business start-ups end in failure within the first 120 (one hundred twenty) days. Yes, you read that right. NINETY PERCENT!

This failure rate should be a warning to those who are considering trying their hand at making a go of working on the Internet rather than at a job in the brick and mortar world.

Of course, success is possible. There IS that other 10% (ten percent) that do succeed. The thing is success doesn't happen by accident. And success isn't just a crap shoot. Success happens because of some very important factors.

Success happens because people have the right ideas about internet marketing and how it works. They do not expect to get rich quick or be able to make a killing over night and retire to a tropical isle.

It is strange but some how the same people who wouldn't dream of starting a real world business, think they can make a go of an internet business even though they have no business background.

People will go into an internet business with the idea that they no longer have to get up and go to work. They think they can simply work when the feel like it and still make a good living. They simply do not expect to have to work hard or work long hours.

Wrong Perceptions about the Internet

The 90% failure rate of new Internet businesses really isn't all that surprising when you stop to think about the people who are starting internet businesses.

For some unknown reason most people think that running a successful internet business is as easy as getting a website built and hanging out an 'open for business' sign. They couldn't be more wrong.

The Rules Of Successful Entrepreneurs

Running a successful internet business of any kind requires self-discipline. People will start an internet business and think that they can party all night, sleep until noon and then make a living in 3 or 4 hours sitting in front of a computer. They some how think that the world is just going to line up on their website and hand over money. It isn't going to happen.

Internet businesses do not run on auto-pilot. It is true that well established internet marketing gurus do not have to put in long, tedious hours on their businesses but it is a privilege that that has been earned by putting in a lot of long and tedious hours.

It didn't happen overnight for them and it won't happen over night for anybody. Most people are totally unprepared for the time investment that must be made in order for an internet business to become successful.

No Business Background

The Rules Of Successful Entrepreneurs

All businesses have two things in common. They are BUSINESSES and they must be run like businesses! The people who are in charge of a business need to understand the accepted practices of business.

They need to understand simple and basic ideas like acceptable over-head expenses in relation to projected income. Internet entrepreneurs need to understand profit and loss and what constitutes each.

A college degree in business in not essential for an internet business entrepreneur go be successful but it sure wouldn't hurt. Just some basic business knowledge is absolutely vital.

f you have a hard time balancing your personal check book, you probably should keep your day job and forget about starting an internet business.

It is true that you can hire accounting firms that will tell you **WHEN** you must make tax deposits, for example, but these firms will not be able to tell you **IF** you need to make them.

The Rules Of Successful Entrepreneurs

Accounting firms can tell you whether or not you made a profit but not how to make it. If you have no business background you need to, at the very minimum, get some good business advice before you even consider opening an online business.

The fact is that all successful businesses operate on sound business principles. Successful businesses aren't accidents. The proof is in the numbers....only 10% of new internet businesses are successful or are even still in existence after the first 120 days of operation.

It is not even reasonable to expect to make a profit from a new business enterprise for many, many months.

You must have sufficient resources available to not only launch your business but provide for your own personal needs for an extended period of time. It's called 'capital' and there is no way around the need for enough of it.

The Right Mindset Just Isn't There!

You have most likely heard the phrase, 'He has an attitude!" This is usually a derogatory remark made about a person with a disagreeable attitude.

But the word 'attitude' is an important one when discussing internet marketing start-ups. A good attitude…a good mind set can't insure success but a bad attitude and a bad mind set can certainly guarantee failure.

Here are some wrong attitudes that will absolutely guarantee failure:

The Rules Of Successful Entrepreneurs

1. **I can work when I want to.** Wrong, wrong, wrong! You can't just work when you feel like it. You have to expect to put in many long and very tedious hours of very hard work to make a new internet enterprise succeed.
2. **I can get rich quick!** You couldn't be more wrong and you are not only wrong but you are putting yourself in danger as well. There are bazillions of crooks out there on the internet who are waiting for their next easy mark and if you are looking for a quick way to get rich, you ARE the next mark.

It is possible to make a very comfortable living with internet marketing enterprises but if anybody ever tells you it is quick or easy, they are lying to you.

1. **I don't need a business plan.** There you are...wrong yet again. Internet business is still business. All of the same business principles apply to online business as apply to brick and mortar business. It is imperative that you have a plan for success that is based upon these sound business principles.

2. **When you have an internet business of your own, you don't have a boss.** Wrong again! You are your boss. If you aren't a good boss who sees to it that work is accomplished on time and in full, you will doom yourself to certain failure. Unless you are a boss who sets up a working schedule and establishes goals that must be met, you will find yourself working at a job under a boss who does do those things and maybe for minimum wage.

How You Can Avoid Joining the Failing Masses

The thing about starting a business...any business.....is that there is no guarantee of success under any circumstances.

The Rules Of Successful Entrepreneurs

Even big international businesses can fail at new business ventures. Failure is always an option but the possibility of success can be optimized.

You can optimize the possibility of success by:

The Rules Of Successful Entrepreneurs

1. **Having a good solid business plan in place BEFORE you launch your online business.** There is an old saying: "Those who fail to plan, plan to fail". A detailed set of plans for success needs to be made. You need to have the steps from getting from point A to point B listed in great detail that include realistic cost estimates for accomplishing each step.

2. **Expecting to work very hard to accomplish your goals.** You must never expect anything to be easy. You will be right most of the time because things are rarely as easy as they look. Each step toward success requires work, time and patience. Sometimes things don't work out right on the first try. You have to be willing to try again and again until you do succeed.

3. **Not falling for 'get-rich-quick schemes.** The internet woods are full of those who prey upon those who are looking for quick and easy ways to become rich. Those ways do not exist. Get over thinking that there is an easy way. There is NOT.

Remember those statistics! Ninety percent of all new internet businesses fail in the first 120 days. You don't have to be part of that majority. You can become a part of that 10% minority of successful internet business enterprises.

Chapter 5: The Cornerstones of Successful Internet Entrepreneurship

Running a successful internet business can look so simple when you are on the outside looking in. You look at a successful internet entrepreneur and he doesn't look like he is doing anything special but he is living the good life. It really doesn't look like he is working all that hard. He seems to be enjoying life immensely.

The Rules Of Successful Entrepreneurs

Really...all he is doing is sitting comfortably in front of his own computer in his own very comfortable home a few hours a day. He talks on the telephone and seems to be enjoying every conversation.

Apparently, running a successful internet business is the proverbial 'piece of cake'! Right? WRONG!!! Wrong, wrong, wrong!

You are looking at the results of a very, very long and tedious process that consisted of many very long, late-night hours and a lot of blood, sweat and tears over a period of several years.

This successful internet entrepreneur worked very, very hard for the success that you are looking at.

It is more than a little bit likely that he first placed four corner stones first as he began the long process of building his successful Internet business. Those four corner stones upon which he built his success are:

1. The right mind set.
2. Recognizing and using leverage.
3. Building a set of useful contacts.
4. And he probably had a mentor.

We will discuss these four corner stones that must be laid down first so that a successful internet business can be constructed.

All of them are important, even crucial to the success of any business but especially to the success of an internet based business.

Constructing a successful business in cyberspace has many things in common with the building of a successful brick and mortar business but there are significant differences as well.

Having the Right, Healthy Mindset

The success of any business both of the online variety as well as the off line variety require the right mindset from the get-go.

A right and healthy mind set will not guarantee success but a wrong and unhealthy or unrealistic mindset will most assuredly guarantee failure. So the right mind set is the first corner stone that must be laid upon which a successful business can be constructed.

What is a right and healthy mindset? There are things that it <u>is</u> as well as things that it <u>isn't</u>.

The Rules Of Successful Entrepreneurs

A right and healthy mindset <u>IS</u> the willingness to work as hard and as long as is necessary to achieve the goals that has been set. A right and healthy mindset <u>ISN'T</u> the belief that success will be easy, quick or painless.

Those who believe that they can make an internet business enterprise thrive without having to actually put in any time or effort are simply doomed to failure from the beginning.

There are schemers and scammers out there in cyberspace that are just waiting eagerly for those to come along who are looking for easy riches.

A right and healthy mindset <u>IS</u> the willingness to take the time to make a good, solid business plan that is based upon sound business principles.

A right and healthy mindset <u>ISN'T</u> just jumping in feet first and hoping for the best. The best that can happen under those circumstances is that you get out with anymore than two cents to your name.

'Flying by the seat of your pants' is NOT a plan…it is just plain suicide in the world of internet marketing. If you don't have a formal education in business, you need to find people who do have that kind of education and seek then follow their advice.

Recognizing and Using Leverage

There are dozens…maybe hundreds….of business models out there. Some are, of course, more successful than others but they all come with their own set of pros and cons.

The idea is to get the most bang for the buck. You need to use all of the power of the Internet to make your e-business successful. You really cannot afford to leave any stone unturned.

If you are a real go-getter, the temptation is to do everything first and that isn't possible. You need to make a realistic plan and build one thing upon another until you have a good solid base from which to operate.

Once you get a website built, you will need to begin leveraging SEO (search engine optimization) and gaining page rank.

The Rules Of Successful Entrepreneurs

One thing does lead to another, of course, but one of the quickest ways to leverage SEO is to add a blog to your website. This is a way that you can get much more quickly indexed by the search engines.

Leveraging also includes branding yourself, your website and your products. One of the quicker ways to begin to get yourself branded is by investing in PLR (Private Label Rights) products and changing the names of those products to include your own name or logo. (Don't forget that there must be some rewriting done.)

This is probably the quickest way to become branded as well as gain credibility on the internet. For example: you might buy a PLR E-Book about Easy Dog Training and change the name to 'John Doe's Easy Dog Training Methods'.

You can sell the book, give it away as a free gift on your own website or list it in E-Book repositories for others to use.

Remember that reputation and credibility are everything on the internet. Don't take any shortcuts and never damage or allow others to damage either.

It Is Not What You Know, But Who You Know

That is an old saying. "It is not <u>What</u> you know, but <u>Who</u> you know that counts". Setting a corner stone of good solid relationships is an important aspect of building a successful e-enterprise.

Working hard at building good solid business relationships is worth every minute of time that you invest in it. Business relationship building should be one of your top priorities.

When you build social relationships, you insert yourself into social situations where you come in contact with people who have interests that are similar to or complimentary to your own interests don't you?

That is precisely the same way that business relationships are established. You insert yourself into business situations where you will meet others who have businesses that are similar to or complimentary to your own business. You develop relationships over a period of time.

There are several ways in which to accomplish this task. One way is to participate in teleseminars or webinars that are related to your business.

You will learn a lot, of course, but equally important, you will come in contact with those who are already succeeding in the niche market that you are working in.

Of course, attending real brick and mortar world seminars is an even better way to begin to build friendly business relationships with not only your peers but also with those who are in a position to help you....which brings me to the final corner stone that you need to lay.

Find a Capable Mentor

It isn't likely that there is a more valuable asset that a new e-entrepreneur can have than a good and capable mentor. Someone who has already made all of the mistakes can help you to avoid making all of the mistakes yourself.

They have the wisdom that comes from experience to point out pitfalls and to help direct you toward the better of choices.

The Rules Of Successful Entrepreneurs

Why, you ask, would anyone who has it made want to take their time to help a newbie succeed?

Maybe I can answer that by telling you about my friend who is an accomplished musician. He played with some of the biggest stars in the business. He is a very, very fine guitarist who is now in his 70's.

He has about three young guitarists that he spends many hours not only teaching how to play but counseling them on career choices.

I asked him why he spent so much time doing that and he said, "It is like gaining immortality. If I teach them and they teach others, then what I know lives forever."

Successful internet marketers want that 'immortality' as well. The ones who are the very most successful are the ones, amazingly enough, who are the most likely to mentor an up and coming e-entrepreneur.

Of course, these successful internet marketers are not going to be interested in wasting their time on a person who has not already worked hard to lay those first three corner stones themselves.

These potential mentors are looking for new comers who show that they have a right and healthy mindset, who are working hard at leveraging and who are well aware of how important it is to know all the players and the RIGHT people.

It short, the new comer most likely to get a mentor is one who is already working hard and helping himself and not looking for someone who can just smooth the way for him.

Chapter 6: The Key to Continuous Growth and Expansion

Grow or die! This is one of the laws of nature that applies to all living things. All business lives by this law as well. A business cannot begin, grow to a certain point and then simply remain at that point and continue to thrive.

Growth and expansion are necessary for the business to survive and if that growth and expansion do not happen then the business will fade and die or crash and burn.

Growth and expansion of business must be controlled by the business owners or managers. If growth is too slow, the business lags behind the competition. If growth is too fast, the business can easily become over extended.

A steady controlled growth is the ideal. Of course, the ideal and the reality are sometimes two very different things.

Sometimes the terms 'growth and expansion' are a bit misunderstood. The most obvious meaning of both terms is to get bigger and broader but those meanings are not the only ones that apply.

Growth, for example, can mean gaining knowledge and becoming wiser and expansion can mean broadening the knowledge base from which a company operates.

The Rules Of Successful Entrepreneurs

A small internet based company does not have to grow and expand until it becomes a giant multi-national company in order to survive but the owners and managers of these internet businesses do have to grow by getting smarter and expand by welcoming change with open arms.

Nothing ever just stays the same. Change is the only certainty in the world. What was hot or what worked yesterday is old news today and it will be ancient history tomorrow.

Companies and company owners and managers must grow with and adapt to changes as they happen and on the internet changes happen a lot faster than they do out in the brick and mortar world.

We all agree that growing, adapting and expanding is vital to the survival of any business and maybe especially to Internet business. So the question is: What is the key to growth and expansion of internet based businesses?

When brick and mortar businesses grow and expand, they build bigger buildings and hire more employees but that isn't exactly an option for an internet based business.

The key to growth and expansion of an internet based business is for the business owner or manager to always and continuously invest in them.

They must be willing to stay on the cutting edge of technology and they must be willing to accept and adapt to changes as they occur.

Internet businesses are not buildings. Internet businesses are people. An internet business cannot grow by investing in a larger building.

It only grows when the person who is driving that business invests in his or her own knowledge and ability.

An internet business cannot expand by investing in hiring more people. An internet business expands when the person who is driving it invests in himself or herself.

The bottom line is this: The key to continuous growth and expansion of an internet based business is continuous investments being made in the owner or manager of the business. The short answer: **Invest in yourself**.

Invest in Yourself

The Rules Of Successful Entrepreneurs

You have no doubt heard this refrain many times.

"Invest in yourself! Invest in yourself! Invest is yourself!" But what does 'invest in yourself mean'? Does it mean you should go out and invest in a haircut that costs two hundred bucks? Does it mean that you should go by yourself a designer suit? What does it mean to invest in yourself?

Well, if you can afford it, go get that haircut and buy that designer suit but that is not the kind of investment that we are talking about here.

Your internet business is just you, your computer and your internet connection and you could actually operate your internet business from any commuter on the planet that had an internet connection.

So basically, your business is really only you. Your business is based only upon your own knowledge and your own ability. Those are the 'company' assets and those are the ones that need to grow and expand constantly so that your internet business thrives.

The Rules Of Successful Entrepreneurs

Here is a rule that you might want to live by to insure that your internet business is a success and continues to be a success: Invest 5% of your time and income into improving your self.

Expansion and growth are imperative to survival and expansion and growth of an internet business means expanding and growing the knowledge of the person running the company...that would be YOU.

A tiny investment of only 5% of your time and your income per year in yourself can mean that you will continue to see positive monetary returns for many, many years to come.

You might be sitting there shaking your head and still wondering what is meant by a 5% time and income investment per year in yourself. What is meant is that you must expand your knowledge.

You must stay on top of new technological advancements and you must expand your knowledge base about your own area of expertise. Things change fast. New information becomes available on almost everything under the sun every day of the week.

It is very, very easy to fall behind very, very quickly. And unless you consciously put forth the effort to stay on top of things you will most certainly fall behind. Keeping up is easier than catching up and if you keep up, you can usually find a way to forge ahead.

Yes, you are so busy right now that you could use 48 hour days but taking just about one hour per day out of the 24 that you are allotted and only $5 out of every hundred dollars that you earn and investing that time and money in yourself can increase your future earnings a hundred fold.

There are newsletters, webinars, teleseminars and real brick and mortar seminars that can provide information and cause your knowledge to grow and expand so that your business can also grow and expand but you must be willing to invest in yourself so that you can take advantage of this information...learn it...and apply it to your own internet business.

Self-Investment Tips that Really Work

The Rules Of Successful Entrepreneurs

It is absolutely true that time is the one commodity that most internet entrepreneurs have a very, very short supply of. Still there are ways to use time that would otherwise be of no value to invest in yourself. Here are a few tips that might help:

Ø Use travel time to invest in yourself. By using your iPod or your MP3 player you can use your travel time to expand your knowledge.

Ø Set your clock for a half hour earlier and use that time to read and learn.

Ø After you stop working in the evening, use your computer to search for new information and ideas.

Of course there are some things that are just going to take your time but you can choose wisely.

Ø Attend webinars and teleseminars that are directly related to your niche or your business.

Ø Attend real world seminars that are closer to your home and will require less travel time but will provide you with the information that you need.

Resist the Urge of Staying in the Comfort Zone

We all have a comfort zone and all of us are very fond of our personal comfort zone. It is very, very tempting to just stick with doing the things that we have always done and doing them in the same way we have always done them.

However, staying in your comfort zone and refusing to expand your mind and your horizons can cause you and your internet business to fail.

There is an old saying (probably made up by someone who was afraid of trying new things) that says, "If it isn't broke, don't fix it." Well, 'it' doesn't have to be broken in order to be improved upon whatever 'it' is.

Candle light wasn't broken but we are all glad that electricity was harnessed. Electric light is still light but it is certainly a big improvement over candle light.

The Rules Of Successful Entrepreneurs

New ideas come along every day in the world of internet business. Some of those ideas are even good ones even if they do reside outside of our own personal comfort zone.

In order to continue to invest in yourself, you must be willing to leave your own comfort zone. Just because what has worked is still working it doesn't mean that there are not newer, better and more efficient ways of doing things.

Nobody is saying that new is always better. New is not always better but sometimes it is and the only way to tell which is which is by investigating new ideas yourself and then adapting the ones that can help you to your business.

Invest in yourself by increasing your knowledge and don't be afraid of trying new things and new ways of doing things. These things really are the secrets of success and not just in the world of internet business but in life itself.

Chapter 7: The Razor Edge Difference Between Work and Deals

Just about every internet marketer that I have ever known has worked at some kind of job other than internet marketing before they launched their internet marketing careers.

It is a funny thing about working at a job that pays you for the work that you do. You get into a 'work-equals- money' mindset. After all, when you work for others, work does, in fact, equal money.

But when you launch an internet marketing career the 'work' that used to make money for you now prevents you from making money.

The Rules Of Successful Entrepreneurs

It is true. The 'work' that you are doing that you once got paid to do, like answering the telephone, answering emails, filing papers, etc. is actually preventing you from making the deals that will put money in your pocket.

Yet we continue to seek work because we are programmed to think of work as the thing that makes money.

We get stuck in the 'work-equals-money' mindset that is actually counter-productive to building a successful internet marketing business.

We focus our time and energy on finding work for ourselves rather than on focusing our time and energy on making the deals that will really make money for us.

It isn't hard to see why we get into this 'work-equals-money' mindset. We have been living with that concept since we were kids.

Think about it. What was your first job? Did you cut grass for a neighbor? Didn't you get money after you had done the work? Of course, you did. He wasn't paying you to think...he was paying you to cut grass.

The Rules Of Successful Entrepreneurs

When you got older and got a job at the local burger joint, you got paid for cooking hamburgers and French Fries. You cooked the hamburgers and fries and then you got paid. Word did in fact equal money.

The owner of the hamburger joint wasn't paying you to find a better way to cook hamburgers or paying you to look for a new market to sell hamburgers. He was only paying you for doing the work of cooking the hamburgers.

But now you are not getting paid for doing the 'work'. The work isn't what is making money for you.

It is true that the work must still be done but you don't have to look for it. It will find you. What you need to be looking for now are the deals that will make you money.

What Constitutes Work?

What is 'work'? The 'work' that makes any business work is just the day to day activities that must be accomplished in order for the business to function. Telephone calls must be answered.

Emails must be read and responded to. Files must be kept orderly. The list goes on and on but this is just 'work'.

Nobody is going to pay you to answer the phone, read emails or keep files in order. That is simply 'work' that must be done. It isn't making you any money and it most certainly is not what you should be focused upon.

Once an internet marketing business has gotten up and running, it is a very good investment to simply pay a virtual assistant to do the 'work' and set yourself free to make the deals that actually make you money and make your internet marketing business thrive.

You can't do this right away, of course, but you can use as little of your time as possible on mundane tasks.

The Rules Of Successful Entrepreneurs

You can spend hours and hours and hours of your time working on your website....making it better...tweaking this and tweaking that. That is work that is not putting a single red cent into your bank account.

Hire a techie to do that 'work' for you while you are making deals that make more than enough to pay the techie.

Until you can hire someone to do this work for you, get it fixed as best you can and move on the productive deal making.

How many hours are you spending each day writing and making posts to your blogs? Is this time actually making any money for you?

No, of course, it isn't. It is just 'work'. It is work that others could do just as well or work that you can find ways to make shorter like by using PLR materials rather than writing every word yourself.

Customer service is absolutely vital work that must be done. It must be done quickly and efficiently and above all competently.

It might even be work that in the beginning at least that you must do yourself.

There are however companies and individuals out there in cyber space that are perfectly capable of handling this work for you and you don't have to make it harder than it needs to be.

What Constitutes Making Deals?

Yes, it is absolutely true that the 'work' must be done, but the work that must be done should be done as quickly and as efficiently as possible and you shouldn't concentrate your energy on finding and creating more work that isn't going to making any money for you.

You need to be focusing your attention on making the deals that will make money.

Just as soon as you possibly can, you should begin to hire people to do the mundane tasks that must be accomplished and free up as much of your own time as possible for deal making.

So what exactly are the activities that constitute deal making? Briefly and concisely they are the activities that have the potential for putting money into your bank account. A few of these activities are:

1. **Visiting forums and blogs that relate to your niche**: Forums and blogs are where you find the real living, breathing people who are YOUR potential customers and until somebody drags out their credit card, puts in their information and actually buys products or services from you, you haven't made a dime so you need to go where the people are and find out how to best serve their wants and needs.

2. **Visit websites that are related to your website**. This is where you will find your potential joint venture partners. Contact the webmasters and work on making mutually profitable deals.

3. **Start your own newsletter or E-zine**: This is one of the most potentially profitable deals that you can make for yourself. The longer your list grows, the more profits you can make.

4. **Attend seminars in the brick and mortar world and build good solid business relationships with others in your field**. Here again are potential joint venture partners that you need to take the time to cultivate.

5. **Put together your own webinar or teleseminar**: Find interesting speakers who would supply information of interest to your list. Webinars and teleseminars are both easy and inexpensive to do and are both money making deals that you can make.

Does this Mean We Should Ditch Work And Focus On Entirely Deals Only?

It would really be nice if we could just ditch the work-a-day-work and do nothing with our time other than make the deals that make us money! Now that would be what I would call a perfect world.

Unfortunately, the work-a-day-work must be done and until our 'ship comes in' we are probably going to be the ones who have to do that as well as make the deals that make us money.

As long as we are going to have to do both we can at least learn how to work smarter. We can learn how to get the same amount of 'work' accomplished in less time so that we can free up more time for making the deals that will make us money.

The Rules Of Successful Entrepreneurs

Some examples of working smarter are:

1. Write a FAQ page for your website and use your autoresponder to direct most questions to that site.
2. Subscribe to a Private Label Rights (PLR) membership website and use that material (with only a little rewrite) as your blog posts and your website content. You can even make whole new products that can be sold from this PLR material.
3. Make a schedule for yourself that allows only so much time for the tasks that must be completed that make you no money and allow more time in that schedule for the deal making tasks that will make you money.
4.
5. Invest in automation software that is designed to take care of simple every day but time consuming tasks.

There is always the 'work' that must be done each and every day but don't let it become the object of your focus. Don't look for work to be done. Work no longer equals money for you now that you are an internet marketer.

Get the work done as quickly as you can and put your focus on the deal making activities that will add to your bottom line. It is no longer your job just to make hamburgers...now you need to get out there and look for new markets. You ARE getting paid to think now.

Chapter 8: It's Your Call Now: Take Action!

The success (or failure) of your Internet Entrepreneurship really is up to you now. If you succeed, the credit will all belong to you and if you fail, you will own that as well. Your success or failure is in your own hands.

Success and failure are two sides of the same coin. The coin in question is your own Internet Entrepreneurship and you don't want to flip that coin into the air and leave it to chance as to whether it lands on success or failure.

You want complete control over the fate of your Internet business and you do have that control.

Every decision will be yours to make.

If you make wise choices then you will claim victory and success will be yours.

If you make unwise choices then your internet business will crash and burn and your own hopes and dreams will go up in flames along with it.

Beating the Odds

You do realize, of course, that the odds for success are not in your favor. Every day thousands and thousands of internet business enterprises are launched. Of those internet businesses that will be launched today, 90% (ninety percent) will not be around in 120 days.

That is right! You have no better than a 10% chance of actually making a success out of your internet business unless you can change them those are not very good odds. If it were a horse race, winning would be considered a long shot.

That is the down side but anytime there is a down side there is always an up side.

The upside in this case is that even though you have only a 10% chance at succeeding, you can greatly better your odds by simply following the guidelines that have already been offered.

You can increase your odds from 10% to 90% by simply applying a few very simple principles to the problem.

The reasons that so many new Internet entrepreneurs fail within the first 120 days can be narrowed down to four.

1. They do not have the right mindset.
2. They do not lay a solid foundation.
3. They do not have the key to unlock growth and expansion.
4. They do not plan for success

The Right Mindset for Success

Unfortunately, so many people think that they can quit their jobs, open an internet business and just relax and enjoy life. They expect instant success and instant wealth without having to invest anything (even time and effort) to affect that success.

The Rules Of Successful Entrepreneurs

They really believe that they can sleep until noon, work when and if they want to and just rack up sales and profit. This attitude probably accounts for at least half of all of the failures of new internet businesses.

Making an internet business successful takes a lot of time and even more work. That old real world job demanded that you be on the job for probably 40 hours each week.

Your net internet business will need about twice that many hours each week if it is to become successful. Very, very, very few people are willing to invest that much time and effort thus the 90% failure rate.

Of the few that are willing to put in enough time and effort most expect instant success.

They don't even consider the fact that they will need to continue to meet their own personal expenses for many months before they see the first penny of profit from a new internet business even though those facts are readily available.

These are the ones who go out there looking for get-rich-quick schemes and end up becoming victims of internet scam artists.

The right mindset is this: You must expect to work hard. You must expect to work long and tedious hours. You will not be an over-night success. People are not going to line up to give you their money. You are going to have to earn it.

Laying a Sound Foundation

Sometimes people will start an internet business that has no business background at all. This is another reason for the high failure rate of new internet entrepreneurships.

If you do not have an education in business, then you would be very wise indeed to speak with those who are well versed in business.

An internet business of any kind is a BUSINESS. It must be run like a business and it must be build upon sound business practices. The only 'dumb' questions are those that are never asked.

You need information and the best way there is to get the information that you need is to simply ask questions of those who have the answers.

There are courses available both out in the brick and mortar world as well as on the internet about how to set up and run a successful business.

You can't abide by the rules if you don't know what the rules are. Do your homework before you launch you business.

You need to lay a rock solid foundation so that your new business doesn't become one of the casualties that are caused by poor planning or even no planning. You need a business plan.

You need a business model and it needs to be one that you can understand and follow. Jumping in and hoping for the best isn't a plan. That will only insure that your new internet business will not still be in existence four months from now.

Unlocking Growth and Expansion

Nothing in this world ever stays the same. The only absolute certainty is change. Internet business is not an exception to this rule. As a matter of fact, business on the internet changes faster than just about anything you can imagine.

The Rules Of Successful Entrepreneurs

Another reason that so many new internet businesses don't survive for very long is that a new e-entrepreneur will start a business based upon one single idea and never grow or expand beyond that single idea.

These people have what I sometimes call 'tunnel vision'. They don't look around at the internet business landscape and make the necessary changes that keep them visible and a player in the market place.

Internet businesses themselves will naturally grow and expand if the owner or manager of the business grows and expands his knowledge and is willing to adapt to the inevitable changes that take place on a daily basis in Internet business.

It is simply good business to invest a minimum of 5% of your time and your income back into yourself. You ARE your business.

I've heard the term 'continuing education' tossed about like it was a choice to be made.

The Rules Of Successful Entrepreneurs

Continuing education is not a choice if a business is to be successful. The 10% of new internet businesses that will still be around after the next 120 days will be owned or managed by people who are constantly learning new things and applying those new things to the internet businesses that they operate.

They attend real world seminars. They attend teleseminars and webinars. They read multiple newsletters every single day.

They learn...they grow....they adapt....they succeed. That is very easy to say but it is much harder to accomplish. However, those who do accomplish it will still be in business when most others are not.

Planning Success

There is an old saying that I quote very often. "Those who fail to plan, plan to fail!" I say it often because it is the single most important fact of success in a nutshell.

A plan for an internet business is just exactly like a road map that would be used for making a road trip.

The Rules Of Successful Entrepreneurs

It is a detailed plan of how to get from point A (starting an internet business) to point B (having a successful internet business) in the shortest possible time and without taking the scenic route.

Most of the time those who begin new internet businesses have been working at jobs for which they were paid a salary. They are in the 'work equals money' mindset and they bring that mindset into their internet businesses.

They will even spend their time searching for more 'work' to do rather than searching for ways in which to make money.

Unless the 'work = money' mindset can be quickly changed to 'sales = money' mindset, the business will certainly fail and fail very quickly.

One of the most important items that can be listed in a business plan is to 'find a mentor'. You can have all of the details written down of exactly how you plan to succeed but if you can find a mentor that process can be cut in half.

Of course, it is very unlikely that you will find a mentor within the first 120 days of starting your new internet business but that item needs to always be in your mind as you make contacts and build business relationships.

Building and internet business is a very exciting undertaking but it is one that is fraught with obstacles. You can overcome the obstacles and succeed but don't expect it to be easy or quick. It will be neither.

Chapter 9:
The Golden rules Of Acquiring Wealth

In the United States where there is more land than people, it is not at all difficult for persons in good health to make money. In this comparatively new field there are so many avenues of success open, so many vocations which are not crowded, that any person of either sex who is willing, at least for the time being, to engage in any respectable occupation that offers, may find lucrative employment.

Those who really desire to attain independence, have only to set their minds upon it, and adopt the proper means, as they do in regard to any other object which they wish to accomplish, and the thing is easily done.
as plain as the road to the mill."

simply in expending less than we earn; that seems to be a very simple problem. Mr. Micawber, one of those happy creations of the genial Dickens, puts the case in a strong light when he says that to have annual income of twenty pounds per annum, and spend twenty pounds and sixpence, is to be the most miserable of men; whereas, to have an income of only twenty pounds, and spend but nineteen pounds and sixpence is to be the happiest of mortals. Many of my readers may say, "

But however easy it may be found to make money, I have no doubt many of my hearers will agree it is the most difficult thing in the world to keep it. The road to wealth is, as Dr. Franklin truly says, " *we understand this: this is economy, and we know economy is wealth; we know we can't eat our cake and keep it also.*" Yet perhaps more cases of failure arise from mistakes on this point than almost any other. **The fact is, many people think they understand economy when they really do not.**

True economy is misapprehended, and people go through life without properly comprehending what that principle is. One says, "*I have an income of so much, and here is my neighbor who has the same; yet every year he gets something ahead and I fall short; why is it? I know all about economy.*" He thinks he does, but he does not. There are men who think that economy consists in saving cheese-parings and candle-ends, in cutting off two pence from the laundress' bill and doing all sorts of little, mean, dirty things. **Economy is not meanness.** The misfortune is, also, that this class of persons let their economy apply in only one direction. They fancy they are so wonderfully economical in saving a half-penny where they ought to spend two pence, that they think they can afford to squander in other directions.

Before kerosene oil was discovered or thought of, one might stop overnight at almost any farmer's house in the agricultural districts and get a very good supper, but after supper he might attempt to read in the sitting-room, and would find it impossible with the inefficient light of one candle. The hostess, seeing his dilemma, would say: "*It is rather difficult to read here evenings; the proverb says 'you must have a ship at sea in order to be able to burn two candles at once; we never have an extra candle except on extra occasions.*" These extra occasions occur, perhaps, twice a year. In this way the good woman saves five, six, or ten dollars in that time: but the information which might be derived from having the extra light would, of course, far outweigh a ton of candles.

But the trouble does not end here. Feeling that she is so economical in tallow candies, she thinks she can afford to go frequently to the village and spend twenty or thirty dollars for ribbons and furbelows, many of which are not necessary. This false connote might frequently be seen in men of business, and in those instances it often runs to writing paper. You find good businessmen who save all the old envelopes and scraps, and would not tear a new sheet of paper, if they could avoid it, for the world. This is all very well; they may in this way save five or ten dollars a year, but being so economical (only in note paper), they think they can afford to waste time; to have expensive parties, and to drive their carriages. This is an illustration of' Dr. Franklin's "*saving at the spigot and wasting at the bung-hole,*" "*penny wise and pound foolish.*" Punch in speaking of this "one idea" class of people says "*they are like the man who bought a penny herring for his family's dinner and then hired a coach and four to take it home.*" I never knew a man to succeed by practicing this kind of economy.

True economy consists in always making **the income exceed the out-go**. Wear the old clothes a little longer if necessary; dispense with the new pair of gloves; mend the old dress: live on plainer food if need be; so that, under all circumstances, unless some unforeseen accident occurs, there will be a margin in favor of the income. A penny here, and a dollar there, placed at interest, goes on accumulating, and in this way the desired result is attained. It requires some training, perhaps, to accomplish this economy, but when once used to it, you will find there is more satisfaction in rational saving than in irrational spending.

The Rules Of Successful Entrepreneurs

Here is a recipe which I recommend: **I have found it to work an excellent cure for extravagance, and especially for mistaken economy**. When you find that you have no surplus at the end of the year, and yet have a good income, I advise you to take a few sheets of paper and form them into a book and mark down every item of expenditure. Post it every day or week in two columns, one headed "necessaries" or even "comforts", and the other headed "luxuries," and you will find that the latter column will be double, treble, and frequently ten times greater than the former. The real comforts of life cost but a small portion of what most of us can earn. *It is the eyes of others and not our own eyes which ruin us. If all the world were blind except myself I should not care for fine clothes or furniture.*" In America many persons like to repeat "we are all free and equal," but it is a great mistake in more senses than one.

That we are born "free and equal" is a glorious truth in one sense, yet we are not all born equally rich, and we never shall be.

The Rules Of Successful Entrepreneurs

One may say; "*there is a man who has an income of fifty thousand dollars per annum, while I have but one thousand dollars; I knew that fellow when he was poor like myself; now he is rich and thinks he is better than I am; I will show him that I am as good as he is; I will go and buy a horse and buggy; no, I cannot do that, but I will go and hire one and ride this afternoon on the same road that he does, and thus prove to him that I am as good as he is.*"

My friend, you need not take that trouble; you can easily prove that you are "as good as he is;" you have only to behave as well as he does; but you cannot make anybody believe that you are rich as he is. Besides, if you put on these "airs," add waste your time and spend your money, your poor wife will be obliged to scrub her fingers off at home, and buy her tea two ounces at a time, and everything else in proportion, in order that you may keep up "appearances," and, after all, deceive nobody. On the other hand, Mrs. Smith may say that her next-door neighbor married Johnson for his money, and "everybody says so." She has a nice one-thousand dollar camel's hair shawl, and she will make Smith get her an imitation one, and she will sit in a pew right next to her neighbor in church, in order to prove that she is her equal.

The Rules Of Successful Entrepreneurs

My good woman, you will not get ahead in the world, if your vanity and envy thus take the lead. In this country, where we believe the majority ought to rule, we ignore that principle in regard to fashion, and let a handful of people, calling themselves the aristocracy, run up a false standard of perfection, and in endeavoring to rise to that standard, we constantly keep ourselves poor; all the time digging away for the sake of outside appearances. How much wiser to be a "law unto ourselves" and say, "we will regulate our out-go by our income, and lay up something for a rainy day." People ought to be as sensible on the subject of money-getting as on any other subject. Like causes produces like effects. You cannot accumulate a fortune by taking the road that leads to poverty. It needs no prophet to tell us that those who live fully up to their means, without any thought of a reverse in this life, can never attain a pecuniary independence.

Men and women accustomed to gratify every whim and caprice, will find it hard, at first, to cut down their various unnecessary expenses, and will feel it a great self-denial to live in a smaller house than they have been accustomed to, with less expensive furniture, less company, less costly clothing, fewer servants, a less number of balls, parties, theater-goings, carriage-ridings, pleasure excursions, cigar-smokings, liquor-drinkings, and other extravagances; but, after all, if they will try the plan of laying by a "nest-egg," or, in other words, a small sum of money, at interest or judiciously invested in land, they will be surprised at the pleasure to be derived from constantly adding to their little "pile," as well as from all the economical habits which are engendered by this course.

The old suit of clothes, and the old bonnet and dress, will answer for another season; the Croton or spring water taste better than champagne; a cold bath and a brisk walk will prove more exhilarating than a ride in the finest coach; a social chat, an evening's reading in the family circle, or an hour's play of "hunt the slipper" and "blind man's buff" will be far more pleasant than a fifty or five hundred dollar party, when the reflection on the difference in cost is indulged in by those who begin to know the pleasures of saving. Thousands of men are kept poor, and tens of thousands are made so after they have acquired quite sufficient to support them well through life, in consequence of laying their plans of living on too broad a platform. Some families expend as much as **twenty thousand dollars per annum**, and some <u>much more</u>, and would scarcely know how to live on less, while others secure more solid enjoyment frequently on a twentieth part of that amount. Prosperity is a more severe ordeal than adversity, especially sudden prosperity. "Easy come, easy go," is an old and true proverb. A spirit of pride and vanity, when permitted to have full sway, is the undying canker-worm which gnaws the very vitals of a man's worldly possessions, let them be small or great, hundreds, or millions. Many persons, as they begin to prosper, immediately expand their ideas and commence expending for luxuries, until in a short time their expenses swallow up their income, and they become ruined in their ridiculous attempts to keep up appearances, and make a "sensation."

The Rules Of Successful Entrepreneurs

A gentleman of fortune who says, that when he first began to prosper, his wife would have a new and elegant sofa. "That sofa," he says, "cost me thirty thousand dollars!" When the sofa reached the house, it was found necessary to get chairs to match; then side-boards, carpets and tables "to correspond" with them, and so on through the entire stock of furniture; when at last it was found that the house itself was quite too small and old-fashioned for the furniture, and a new one was built to correspond with the new purchases; "thus," added my friend, "summing up an outlay of thirty thousand dollars, caused by that single sofa, and saddling on me, in the shape of servants, equipage, and the necessary expenses attendant upon keeping up a fine 'establishment,' a yearly outlay of eleven thousand dollars, and a tight pinch at that: whereas, ten years ago, we lived with much more real comfort, because with much less care, on as many hundreds. The truth is," he continued, "that sofa would have brought me to inevitable bankruptcy, had not a most unexampled title to prosperity kept me above it, and had I not checked the natural desire to 'cut a dash'."

The Rules Of Successful Entrepreneurs

The foundation of success in life is good health: that is the substratum fortune; it is also the basis of happiness. A person cannot accumulate a fortune very well when he is sick. He has no ambition; no incentive; no force. Of course, there are those who have bad health and cannot help it: you cannot expect that such persons can accumulate wealth, but there are a great many in poor health who need not be so.

The Rules Of Successful Entrepreneurs

If, then, sound health is the foundation of success and happiness in life, how important it is that we should study the laws of health, which is but another expression for the laws of nature! The nearer we keep to the laws of nature, the nearer we are to good health, and yet how many persons there are who pay no attention to natural laws, but absolutely transgress them, even against their own natural inclination. We ought to know that the "sin of ignorance" is never winked at in regard to the violation of nature's laws; their infraction always brings the penalty. A child may thrust its finger into the flames without knowing it will burn, and so suffers, repentance, even, will not stop the smart. Many of our ancestors knew very little about the principle of ventilation. They did not know much about oxygen, whatever other "gin" they might have been acquainted with; and consequently they built their houses with little seven-by-nine feet bedrooms, and these good old pious Puritans would lock themselves up in one of these cells, say their prayers and go to bed. In the morning they would devoutly return thanks for the "preservation of their lives," during the night, and nobody had better reason to be thankful. Probably some big crack in the window, or in the door, let in a little fresh air, and thus saved them.

The Rules Of Successful Entrepreneurs

Many persons knowingly **violate** the laws of nature against their better impulses, **for the sake of fashion**. For instance, there is one thing that nothing living except a vile worm ever naturally loved, and that is tobacco; yet how many persons there are who deliberately train an unnatural appetite, and overcome this implanted aversion for tobacco, to such a degree that they get to love it. They have got hold of a poisonous, filthy weed, or rather that takes a firm hold of them. Here are married men who run about spitting tobacco juice on the carpet and floors, and sometimes even upon their wives besides. They do not kick their wives out of doors like drunken men, but their wives, I have no doubt, often wish they were outside of the house. Another perilous feature is that this artificial appetite, like jealousy, "grows by what it feeds on;" when you love that which is unnatural, a stronger appetite is created for the hurtful thing than the natural desire for what is harmless. There is an old proverb which says that "habit is second nature," but an artificial habit is stronger than nature. Take for instance, an old tobacco-chewer; his love for the "quid" is stronger than his love for any particular kind of food. He can give up roast beef easier than give up the weed.

The Rules Of Successful Entrepreneurs

Young lads regret that they are not men; they would like to go to bed boys and wake up men; and to accomplish this they copy the bad habits of their seniors. Little Tommy and Johnny see their fathers or uncles smoke a pipe, and they say, "If I could only do that, I would be a man too; uncle John has gone out and left his pipe of tobacco, let us try it." They take a match and light it, and then puff away. "We will learn to smoke; do you like it Johnny?" That lad dolefully replies: "Not very much; it tastes bitter;" by and by he grows pale, but he persists arid he soon offers up a sacrifice on the altar of fashion; but the boys stick to it and persevere until at last they conquer their natural appetites and become the victims of acquired tastes.

The Rules Of Successful Entrepreneurs

Take the tobacco-chewer. In the morning, when he gets up, he puts a quid in his mouth and keeps it there all day, never taking it out except to exchange it for a fresh one, or when he is going to eat; oh! yes, at intervals during the day and evening, many a chewer takes out the quid and holds it in his hand long enough to take a drink, and then pop it goes back again. This simply proves that the appetite for rum is even stronger than that for tobacco. When the tobacco-chewer goes to your country seat and you show him your grapery and fruit house, and the beauties of your garden, when you offer him some fresh, ripe fruit, and say, "My friend, I have got here the most delicious apples, and pears, and peaches, and apricots; I have imported them from Spain, France and Italy—just see those luscious grapes; there is nothing more delicious nor more healthy than ripe fruit, so help yourself; I want to see you delight yourself with these things;" he will roll the dear quid under his tongue and answer, "No, I thank you, I have got tobacco in my mouth."

The Rules Of Successful Entrepreneurs

His palate has become narcotized by the noxious weed, and he has lost, in a great measure, the delicate and enviable taste for fruits. This shows what expensive, useless and injurious habits men will get into. I speak from experience. I have smoked until I trembled like an aspen leaf, the blood rushed to my head, and I had a palpitation of the heart which I thought was heart disease, till I was almost killed with fright. When I consulted my physician, he said "break off tobacco using." I was not only injuring my health and spending a great deal of money, but I was setting a bad example. I obeyed his counsel. No young man in the world ever looked so beautiful, as he thought he did, behind a fifteen cent cigar or a meerschaum!

The Rules Of Successful Entrepreneurs

These remarks apply with tenfold force to the use of intoxicating drinks. To make money, requires a clear brain. A man has got to see that two and two make four; he must lay all his plans with reflection and forethought, and closely examine all the details and the ins and outs of business. As no man can succeed in business unless he has a brain to enable him to lay his plans, and reason to guide him in their execution, so, no matter how bountifully a man may be blessed with intelligence, if the brain is muddled, and his judgment warped by intoxicating drinks, it is impossible for him to carry on business successfully. How many good opportunities have passed, never to return, while a man was sipping a "social glass," with his friend! How many foolish bargains have been made under the influence of the "nervine," which temporarily makes its victim think he is rich. How many important chances have been put off until to-morrow, and then forever, because the wine cup has thrown the system into a state of lassitude, neutralizing the energies so essential to success in business. Verily, "wine is a mocker

" The use of intoxicating drinks as a beverage, is as much an infatuation, as is the smoking of opium by the Chinese, and the former is quite as destructive to the success of the business man as the latter. It is an unmitigated evil, utterly indefensible in the light of philosophy; religion or good sense. It is the parent of nearly every other evil in our country.

DON'T MISTAKE YOUR VOCATION

The safest plan, and the one most sure of success for the young man starting in life, is to select the vocation which is most congenial to his tastes. Parents and guardians are often quite too negligent in regard to this. It very common for a father to say, for example: "I have five boys. I will make Billy a clergyman; John a lawyer; Tom a doctor, and Dick a farmer." He then goes into town and looks about to see what he will do with Sammy. He returns home and says "Sammy, I see watch-making is a nice genteel business; I think I will make you a goldsmith." He does this, regardless of Sam's natural inclinations, or genius.

The Rules Of Successful Entrepreneurs

We are all, no doubt, **born for a wise purpose**. There is as much diversity in our brains as in our countenances. Some are born natural mechanics, while some have great aversion to machinery. Let a dozen boys of ten years get together, and you will soon observe two or three are "whittling" out some ingenious device; working with locks or complicated machinery. When they were but five years old, their father could find no toy to please them like a puzzle. They are natural mechanics; but the other eight or nine boys have different aptitudes. I belong to the latter class; I never had the slightest love for mechanism; on the contrary, I have a sort of abhorrence for complicated machinery. I never had ingenuity enough to whittle a cider tap so it would not leak. I never could make a pen that I could write with, or understand the principle of a steam engine. If a man was to take such a boy as I was, and attempt to make a watchmaker of him, the boy might, after an apprenticeship of five or seven years, be able to take apart and put together a watch; but all through life he would be working up hill and seizing every excuse for leaving his work and idling away his time. Watch making is repulsive to him.

Unless a man enters upon the vocation intended for him by nature, and best suited to his peculiar genius, he cannot succeed. I am glad to believe that the majority of persons do find their right vocation. Yet we see many who have mistaken their calling, from the blacksmith up (or down) to the clergyman. You will see, for instance, that extraordinary linguist the "learned blacksmith," who ought to have been a teacher of languages; and you may have seen lawyers, doctors and clergymen who were better fitted by nature for the anvil or the lap stone.

RIGHT PLACE, RIGHT TIME

After securing the right location, you must be careful to select the proper location. You may have been cut out for a hotel keeper, and they say it requires a genius to "know how to keep a hotel." You might conduct a hotel like clock-work, and provide satisfactorily for five hundred guests every day; yet, if you should locate your house in a small village where there is no railroad communication or public travel, the location would be your ruin.

It is equally important that you do not commence business where there are already enough to meet all demands in the same occupation.

AVOID DEBT LIKE A PLAGUE

Young men starting in life should avoid running into debt. That's a given. There is scarcely anything else that drags a person down like debt. It is a slavish position to get ill, yet we find many a young man, hardly out of his "teens," running in debt (and yes, this has been going on for centuries as long as men and history could remember). He meets a chum and says, "Look at this: I have got trusted for a new suit of clothes." He seems to look upon the clothes as so much given to him; well, it frequently is so, but, if he succeeds in paying and then gets trusted again, he is adopting a habit which will keep him in poverty through life. **Debt robs a man of his self-respect, and makes him almost despise himself**.

Grunting and groaning and working for what he has eaten up or worn out, and now when he is called upon to pay up, he has nothing to show for his money; this is properly termed "working for a dead horse." I do not speak of merchants buying and selling on credit, or of those who buy on credit in order to turn the purchase to a profit.

Money is in some respects like fire; it is a very excellent servant but a terrible master. When you have it mastering you; when interest is constantly piling up against you, it will keep you down in the worst kind of slavery. But let money work for you, and you have the most devoted servant in the world. It is no "eye-servant." There is nothing animate or inanimate that will work so faithfully as money when placed at interest, well secured. It works night and day, and in wet or dry weather.

So do not let it work against you; if you do there is no chance for success in life so far as money is concerned.

PERSEVERENCE IS REALLY ANOTHER WORD FOR SELF-RELIANCE

The Rules Of Successful Entrepreneurs

When a man is in the right path, he must persevere. I speak of this because there are some persons who are "born tired;" naturally lazy and possessing no self-reliance and no perseverance. But they can cultivate these qualities, as Davy Crockett said:

"*This thing remember, when I am dead: Be sure you are right, then go ahead.*"

It is this go-ahead addiction, this determination not to let the horrors or the blues take possession of you, so as to make you relax your energies in the struggle for independence, which you must cultivate.

How many have almost reached the goal of their ambition, but, losing faith in themselves, have relaxed their energies, and the golden prize has been lost forever.

It is, no doubt, often true, as Shakespeare says:

"*There is a tide in the affairs of men, Which, taken at the flood, leads on to fortune.*"

If you hesitate, some bolder hand will stretch out before you and get the prize. Remember the proverb of Solomon: "*He becometh poor that dealeth with a slack hand; but the hand of the diligent maketh rich.*"

Perseverance is sometimes but another word for **self-reliance**. Many persons naturally look on the dark side of life, and borrow trouble. They are born so. Then they ask for advice, and they will be governed by one wind and blown by another, and cannot rely upon themselves. Until you can get so that you can rely upon yourself, you need not expect to succeed.

Men who have met with pecuniary reverses, and absolutely committed suicide, because they thought they could never overcome their misfortune. But I have known others who have met more serious financial difficulties, and have bridged them over by simple perseverance, aided by a firm belief that they were doing justly, and that Providence would "*overcome evil with good.*"

You will see this illustrated in any sphere of life.

WHATEVER YOU DO, DO IT WITH ALL YOUR MIGHT

The Rules Of Successful Entrepreneurs

Work at it, if necessary, early and late, in season and out of season, not leaving a stone unturned, and never deferring for a single hour that which can be done just as well now. The old proverb is full of truth and meaning, "Whatever is worth doing at all, is worth doing well." Many a man acquires a fortune by doing his business thoroughly, while his neighbor remains poor for life, because he only half does it. Ambition, energy, industry, perseverance, are indispensable requisites for success in business.

Fortune always favors the brave, and never helps a man who does not help himself. It won't do to spend your time like Mr. Micawber, in waiting for something to "turn up." To such men one of two things usually "turns up:" the poorhouse or the jail; for idleness breeds bad habits, and clothes a man in rags. The poor spendthrift vagabond says to a rich man:

"I have discovered there is enough money in the world for all of us, if it was equally divided; this must be done, and we shall all be happy together."

"But," was the response, "if everybody was like you, it would be spent in two months, and what would you do then?"

"Oh! Divide again; keep dividing, of course!"

I was recently reading in a London paper an account of a like philosophic pauper who was kicked out of a cheap boarding-house because he could not pay his bill, but he had a roll of papers sticking out of his coat pocket, which, upon examination, proved to be his plan for paying off the national debt of England without the aid of a penny.

People have got to do as Cromwell said: "not only trust in Providence, but keep the powder dry." Do your part of the work, or you cannot succeed. Mahomet, one night, while encamping in the desert, overheard one of his fatigued followers remark: "I will loose my camel, and trust it to God!" "No, no, not so," said the prophet, "tie thy camel, and trust it to God!" Do all you can for yourselves, and then trust to Providence, or luck, or whatever you please to call it, for the rest.

DEPEND UPON YOUR OWN PERSONAL EXERTIONS

The eye of the employer is often worth <u>more</u> than the hands of a dozen employees.

The Rules Of Successful Entrepreneurs

In the nature of things, an agent cannot be so faithful to his employer as to himself. Many who are employers will call to mind instances where the best employees have overlooked important points which could not have escaped their own observation as a proprietor. No man has a right to expect to succeed in life unless he understands his business, and nobody can understand his business thoroughly unless he learns it by personal application and experience. A man may be a manufacturer: he has got to learn the many details of his business personally; he will learn something every day, and he will find he will make mistakes nearly every day. And these very mistakes are helps to him in the way of experiences if he but heeds them. He will be like the Yankee tin-peddler, who, having been cheated as to quality in the purchase of his merchandise, said: "All right, there's a little information to be gained every day; I will never be cheated in that way again." Thus a man buys his experience, and it is the best kind if not purchased at too dear a rate.

Among the maxims of the elder Rothschild was one, all apparent paradox:

The Rules Of Successful Entrepreneurs

"*Be cautious and bold.*" This seems to be a contradiction in terms, but it is not, and there is great wisdom in the maxim. It is, in fact, a condensed statement of what I have already said. It is to say; "you must exercise your caution in laying your plans, but be bold in carrying them out." A man who is all caution, will never dare to take hold and be successful; and a man who is all boldness, is merely reckless, and must eventually fail. A man may go on "'change" and make fifty, or one hundred thousand dollars in speculating in stocks, at a single operation. But if he has simple boldness without caution, it is mere chance, and what he gains to-day he will lose to-morrow. You must have both the caution and the boldness, to insure success.

The Rothschilds have another maxim: "*Never have anything to do with an unlucky man or place.*" (This particular maxim is also discussed in the 48 Laws of Power). That is to say, never have anything to do with a man or place which never succeeds, because, although a man may appear to be honest and intelligent, yet if he tries this or that thing and always fails, it is on account of some fault or infirmity that you may not be able to discover but nevertheless which must exist.

There is <u>no such thing</u> in the world as luck. There never was a man who could go out in the morning and find a purse full of gold in the street to-day, and another to-morrow, and so on, day after day: He may do so once in his life; but so far as mere luck is concerned, he is as liable to lose it as to find it. "Like causes produce like effects." If a man adopts the proper methods to be successful, "luck" will not prevent him. If he does not succeed, there are reasons for it, although, perhaps, he may not be able to see them.

USE THE BEST TOOLS

The Rules Of Successful Entrepreneurs

Men in engaging employees should be careful to get the best. Understand, you cannot have too good tools to work with, and there is no tool you should be so particular about as living tools. If you get a good one, it is better to keep him, than keep changing. He learns something every day; and you arc benefited by the experience he acquires. He is worth more to you this year than last, and he is the last man to part with, provided his habits are good, and he continues faithful. If, as he gets more valuable, he demands an exorbitant increase of salary; on the supposition that you can't do without him, let him go. When and if ever you have such an employee, always discharge him; first, to convince him that his place may be supplied, and second, because he is good for nothing if he thinks he is invaluable and cannot be spared.

But you would keep him, if possible, in order to profit from the result of his experience. An important element in an employee is the brain. You can see bills up, "Hands Wanted," but "hands" are not worth a great deal without "heads."

Those men who have brains and experience are therefore the most valuable and not to be readily parted with; it is better for them, as well as yourself, to keep them, at reasonable advances in their salaries from time to time.

DON'T GET ABOVE YOUR BUSINESS

Young men after they get through their business training, or apprenticeship, instead of pursuing their avocation and rising in their business, will often lie about doing nothing. They say; "I have learned my business, but I am not going to be a hireling; what is the object of learning my trade or profession, unless I establish myself?'"

"Have you capital to start with?"

"No, but I am going to have it."

"How are you going to get it?"

"I will tell you confidentially; I have a wealthy old aunt, and she will die pretty soon; but if she does not, I expect to find some rich old man who will lend me a few thousands to give me a start. If I only get the money to start with I will do well."

The Rules Of Successful Entrepreneurs

There is no greater mistake than when a young man believes he will succeed with borrowed money. **And take note that this kind of conversation is still repeated even into the 21st century**.

Why? Because every man's experience coincides with that of Mr. Astor, who said, "it was more difficult for him to accumulate his first thousand dollars, than all the succeeding millions that made up his colossal fortune." Money is good for nothing unless you know the value of it by experience. Give a boy twenty thousand dollars and put him in business, and the chances are that he will lose every dollar of it before he is a year older. Like buying a ticket in the lottery; and drawing a prize, it is "easy come, easy go." He does not know the value of it; nothing is worth anything, unless it costs effort. Without self-denial and economy; patience and perseverance, and commencing with capital which you have not earned, you are not sure to succeed in accumulating. Young men, instead of "waiting for dead men's shoes," should be up and doing, for there is no class of persons who are so unaccommodating in regard to dying as these rich old people, and it is fortunate for the expectant heirs that it is so.

The Rules Of Successful Entrepreneurs

<u>Nine out of ten</u> of the rich men of our country today, started out in life as poor boys, with determined wills, industry, perseverance, economy and good habits. They went on gradually, made their own money and saved it; and this is the best way to acquire a fortune. Stephen Girard started life as a poor cabin boy, and died worth nine million dollars. A.T. Stewart was a poor Irish boy; and he paid taxes on a million and a half dollars of income, per year. John Jacob Astor was a poor farmer boy, and died worth twenty millions. Cornelius Vanderbilt began life rowing a boat from Staten Island to New York; he presented our government with a steamship worth a million of dollars, and died worth fifty million. "There is no royal road to learning," says the proverb, and I may say it is equally true, "there is no royal road to wealth." But I think there is a royal road to both. The road to learning is a royal one; the road that enables the student to expand his intellect and add every day to his stock of knowledge, until, in the pleasant process of intellectual growth, he is able to solve the most profound problems, to count the stars, to analyze every atom of the globe, and to measure the firmament this is a regal highway, and it is the only road worth traveling.

So in regards to wealth: go on in confidence, study the rules, and above all things, study human nature; for "the proper study of mankind is man," and you will find that while expanding the intellect and the muscles, your enlarged experience will enable you every day to accumulate more and more principal, which will increase itself by interest and otherwise, until you arrive at a state of independence. You will find, as a general thing, that the poor boys get rich and the rich boys get poor.

For instance, a rich man at his decease, leaves a large estate to his family. His eldest sons, who have helped him earn his fortune, know by experience the value of money; and they take their inheritance and add to it. The separate portions of the young children are placed at interest, and the little fellows are patted on the head, and told a dozen times a day, "you are rich; you will never have to work, you can always have whatever you wish, for you were born with a golden spoon in your mouth." The young heir soon finds out what that means; he has the finest dresses and playthings; he is crammed with sugar candies and almost "killed with kindness," and he passes from school to school, petted and flattered. He becomes arrogant and self-conceited, abuses his teachers, and carries everything with a high hand. He knows nothing of the real value of money, having never earned any; but he knows all about the "golden spoon" business. At college, he invites his poor fellow-students to his room, where he "wines and dines" them. He is cajoled and caressed, and called a glorious good follow, because he is so lavish of his money

He gives his game suppers, drives his fast horses, invites his chums to fetes and parties, determined to have lots of "good times." He spends the night in frolics and debauchery, and leads off his companions with the familiar song, "we won't go home till morning." He gets them to join him in pulling down signs, taking gates from their hinges and throwing them into back yards and horse-ponds. If the police arrest them, he knocks them down, is taken to the lockup, and joyfully foots the bills.

"Ah! my boys," he cries, "what is the use of being rich, if you can't enjoy yourself?"

He might more truly say, "if you can't make a fool of yourself," but he is "fast," hates slow things, and doesn't "see it." Young men loaded down with other people's money are almost sure to lose all they inherit, and they acquire all sorts of bad habits which, in the majority of cases, ruin them in health, purse and character. In this country, one generation follows another, and the poor of today are rich in the next generation, or the third. Their experience leads them on, and they become rich, and they leave vast riches to their young children. These children, having been reared in luxury, are inexperienced and get poor; and after long experience another generation comes on and gathers up riches again in turn.

And thus "history repeats itself," and happy is he who by listening to the experience of others avoids the rocks and shoals on which so many have been wrecked.

The Rules Of Successful Entrepreneurs

In this Republican country, the man makes the business. No matter whether he is a blacksmith, a shoemaker, a farmer, banker or lawyer, so long as his business is legitimate, he may be a gentleman. So any "legitimate" business is a double blessing it helps the man engaged in it, and also helps others. The Farmer supports his own family, but he also benefits the merchant or mechanic who needs the products of his farm. The tailor not only makes a living by his trade, but he also benefits the farmer, the clergyman and others who cannot make their own clothing. But all these classes often may be gentlemen.

The great ambition should be to excel all others engaged in the same occupation. The college-student who was about graduating, said to an old lawyer:

"I have not yet decided which profession I will follow. Is your profession full?"

"The basement is much crowded, but there is plenty of room up-stairs," was the witty and truthful reply.

The Rules Of Successful Entrepreneurs

No profession, trade, or calling, is overcrowded in the upper story. Wherever you find the most honest and intelligent merchant or banker, or the best lawyer, the best doctor, the best clergyman, the best shoemaker, carpenter, or anything else, that man is most sought for, and has always enough to do. As a nation, Americans are too superficial— they are striving to get rich quickly, and do not generally do their business as substantially and thoroughly as they should, but whoever excels all others in his own line, if his habits are good and his integrity undoubted, cannot fail to secure abundant patronage, and the wealth that naturally follows. Let your motto then always be "Excelsior," for by living up to it there is no such word as fail.

LEARN SOMETHING USEFUL

Every man should make his son or daughter learn some useful trade or profession, so that in these days of changing fortunes of being rich to-day and poor tomorrow they may have something tangible to fall back upon. This provision might save many persons from misery, who by some unexpected turn of fortune have lost all their means.

LET HOPE PREDOMINATE, BUT BE NOT TOO VISIONARY

Many persons are always kept poor, because they are too visionary. Every project looks to them like certain success, and therefore they keep changing from one business to another, always in hot water, always "under the harrow." The plan of "**counting the chickens before they are hatched**" is an error of ancient date, but it does not seem to improve by age.

DO NOT SCATTER YOUR POWERS

Engage in one kind of business only, and stick to it faithfully until you succeed, or until your experience shows that you should abandon it. A constant hammering on one nail will generally drive it home at last, so that it can be clinched. When a man's undivided attention is centered on one object, his mind will constantly be suggesting improvements of value, which would escape him if his brain was occupied by a dozen different subjects at once. Many a fortune has slipped through a man's fingers became he was engaged in too many occupations at a time. There is good sense in the old caution against having too many irons in the fire at once.

BE SYSTEMATIC

Men should be systematic in their business. A person who does business by rule, having a time and place for everything, doing his work promptly, will accomplish twice as much and with half the trouble of him who does it carelessly and slipshod. By introducing system into all your transactions, doing one thing at a time, always meeting appointments with punctuality, you find leisure for pastime and recreation; whereas the man who only half does one thing, and then turns to something else, and half does that, will have his business at loose ends, and will never know when his day's work is done, for it never will be done. Of course, there is a limit to all these rules. We must try to preserve the happy medium, for there is such a thing as being too systematic. There are men and women, for instance, who put away things so carefully that they can never find them again. It is too much like the "red tape" formality at Washington, and Mr. Dickens' "Circumlocution Office,"—all theory and no result.

READ THE DAILY PAPERS

Always take a trustworthy newspaper, and thus keep thoroughly posted in regard to the transactions of the world. He who is without a newspaper is cut off from his species. In these days of the Internet, many important inventions and improvements in every branch of trade are being made, and he who don't consult the newspapers will soon find himself and his business left out in the cold. Period.

BEWARE OF "OUTSIDE OPERATIONS"

We sometimes see men who have obtained fortunes, suddenly become poor. In many cases, this arises from intemperance, and often from gaming, and other bad habits. Frequently it occurs because a man has been engaged in "outside operations," of some sort. When he gets rich in his legitimate business, he is told of a grand speculation where he can make a score of thousands. He is constantly flattered by his friends, who tell him that he is born lucky, that everything he touches turns into gold. Now if he forgets that his economical habits, his rectitude of conduct and a personal attention to a business which he understood, caused his success in life, he will listen to the siren voices.

A few days elapse and it is discovered he must put in ten thousand dollars more: soon after he is told "it is all right," but certain matters not foreseen, require an advance of twenty thousand dollars more, which will bring him a rich harvest; but before the time comes around to realize, the bubble bursts, he loses all he is possessed of, and then he learns what he ought to have known at the first, that however successful a man may be in his own business, if he turns from that and engages ill a business which he don't understand, he is like Samson when shorn of his locks his strength has departed, and he becomes like other men.

If a man has plenty of money, he ought to invest something in everything that appears to promise success, and that will probably benefit mankind; but let the sums thus invested be moderate in amount, and never let a man foolishly jeopardize a fortune that he has earned m a legitimate way, by investing it m things m which he has had no experience.

DON'T INDORSE WITHOUT SECURITY

The Rules Of Successful Entrepreneurs

No man ought ever to indorse a note or become security, for any man, be it his father or brother, to a greater extent than he can afford to lose and care nothing about, without taking good security. Here is a man that is worth twenty thousand dollars; he is doing a thriving manufacturing or mercantile trade; you are retired and living on your money; he comes to you and says:

"You are aware that I am worth twenty thousand dollars, and don't owe a dollar; if I had five thousand dollars in cash, I could purchase a particular lot of goods and double my money in a couple of months; will you indorse my note for that amount?"

You reflect that he is worth twenty thousand dollars, and you incur no risk by endorsing his note; you like to accommodate him, and you lend your name without taking the precaution of getting security. Shortly after, he shows you the note with your endorsement canceled, and tells you, probably truly, "that he made the profit that he expected by the operation," you reflect that you have done a good action, and the thought makes you feel happy. By and by, the same thing occurs again and you do it again; you have already fixed the impression in your mind that it is perfectly safe to indorse his notes without security.

But the trouble is, this man is getting money too easily. He has only to take your note to the bank, get it discounted and take the cash. He gets money for the time being without effort; without inconvenience to himself. Now mark the result. He sees a chance for speculation outside of his business. A temporary investment of only $10,000 is required. It is sure to come back before a note at the bank would be due. He places a note for that amount before you. You sign it almost mechanically. Being firmly convinced that your friend is responsible and trustworthy; you indorse his notes as a "matter of course."

The Rules Of Successful Entrepreneurs

Unfortunately the speculation does not come to a head quite so soon as was expected, and another $10,000 note must be discounted to take up the last one when due. Before this note matures the speculation has proved an utter failure and all the money is lost. Does the loser tell his friend, the endorser, that he has lost half of his fortune? Not at all. He don't even mention that he has speculated at all. But he has got excited; the spirit of speculation has seized him; he sees others making large sums in this way (we seldom hear of the losers), and, like other speculators, he "looks for his money where he loses it." He tries again. endorsing notes has become chronic with you, and at every loss he gets your signature for whatever amount he wants. Finally you discover your friend has lost all of his property and all of yours. You are overwhelmed with astonishment and grief, and you say "it is a hard thing; my friend here has ruined me," but, you should add, "I have also ruined him." If you had said in the first place, "I will accommodate you, but I never indorse without taking ample security," he could not have gone beyond the length of his tether, and he would never have been tempted away from his legitimate business. It is a very dangerous thing, therefore, at any time, to let people get possession of money too easily; it tempts them to hazardous speculations, if nothing more.

So with the young man starting in business; let him understand the value of money by earning it. When he does understand its value, then grease the wheels a little in helping him to start business, but remember, men who get money with too great facility cannot usually succeed. You must get the first dollars by hard knocks, and at some sacrifice, in order to appreciate the value of those dollars.

ADVERTISE YOUR BUSINESS

We all depend, more or less, upon the public for our support. We all trade with the public—lawyers, doctors, shoemakers, artists, blacksmiths, showmen, opera stagers, railroad presidents, and college professors. Those who deal with the public must be careful that their goods are valuable; that they are genuine, and will give satisfaction. When you get an article which you know is going to please your customers, and that when they have tried it, they will feel they have got their money's worth, then let the fact be known that you have got it. Be careful to advertise it in some shape or other because it is evident that if a man has ever so good an article for sale, and nobody knows it, it will bring him no return.

The Rules Of Successful Entrepreneurs

Where nearly everybody reads, and where newspapers are issued and circulated in editions of five thousand to two hundred thousand, it would be very unwise if this channel was not taken advantage of to reach the public in advertising. A newspaper goes into the family, and is read by wife and children, as well as the head of the home; hence hundreds and thousands of people may read your advertisement, while you are attending to your routine business. Many, perhaps, read it while you are asleep. The whole philosophy of life is, first "sow," then "reap." That is the way the farmer does; he plants his potatoes and corn, and sows his grain, and then goes about something else, and the time comes when he reaps. But he never reaps first and sows afterwards. This principle applies to all kinds of business, and to nothing more eminently than to advertising. If a man has a genuine article, there is no way in which he can reap more advantageously than by "sowing" to the public in this way. He must, of course, have a really good article, and one which will please his customers; anything spurious will not succeed permanently because the public is wiser than many imagine. Men and women are selfish, and we all prefer purchasing where we can get the most for our money and we try to find out where we can most surely do so.

You may advertise a spurious article, and induce many people to call and buy it once, but they will denounce you as an impostor and swindler, and your business will gradually die out and leave you poor. This is right. Few people can safely depend upon chance custom. You all need to have your customers return and purchase again.

So a man who advertises at all must keep it up until the public know who and what he is, and what his business is, or else the money invested in advertising is lost.

Some men have a peculiar genius for writing a striking advertisement, one that will arrest the attention of the reader at first sight. This fact, of course, gives the advertiser a great advantage. Sometimes a man makes himself popular by an unique sign or a curious display in his window.

BE POLITE AND KIND TO YOUR CUSTOMERS

Politeness and civility are the **best capital ever** invested in business. Large stores, gilt signs, flaming advertisements, will all prove unavailing if you or your employees treat your patrons abruptly. The truth is, **the more kind and liberal a man is the more generous will be the patronage bestowed upon him**. Like begets like. The man who gives the greatest amount of goods of a corresponding quality for the least sum (still reserving for himself a profit) will generally succeed best in the long run. This brings us to the golden rule, "*As ye would that men should do to you, do ye also to them*" and they will do better by you than if you always treated them as if you wanted to get the most you could out of them for the least return.

Men who drive sharp bargains with their customers, acting as if they never expected to see them again, will not be mistaken. They will never see them again as customers.

BE CHARITABLE

Of course men should be charitable, **because it is a duty and a pleasure**. But even as a matter of policy, if you possess no higher incentive, you will find that the liberal man will command patronage, while the sordid, uncharitable miser will be avoided.

Solomon says: "*There is that scattereth and yet increaseth; and there is that withholdeth more than meet, but it tendeth to poverty.*" Of course the only true charity is that which is from the heart.

The best kind of charity is to help those who are willing to help themselves. Promiscuous almsgiving, without inquiring into the worthiness of the applicant, is bad in every sense. But to search out and quietly assist those who are struggling for themselves, is the kind that scatter and yet increase. But don't fall into the idea that some persons practice, of giving a prayer instead of a potato, and a benediction instead of bread, to the hungry. It is easier to make Christians with full stomachs than empty.

DON'T BLAB

Some men have a foolish habit of telling their business secrets. If they make money they like to tell their neighbors how it was done. Nothing is gained by this, and often times much is lost. Say nothing about your profits, your hopes, your expectations, your intentions. And this should apply to letters as well as to conversation.

Business men must write letters, but they should be careful what they put in them. If you are losing money, be especially cautious and not tell of it, or you will lose your reputation.

PRESERVE YOUR INTEGRITY

Integrity is more precious than diamonds or rubies. This advice was not only atrociously wicked, but it was the very essence of stupidity: It was as much as to say if you find it difficult to obtain money honestly, you can easily get it dishonestly. **Not to know that the most difficult thing in life is to make money dishonestly!**

Not to know that our prisons are full of men who attempted to follow this advice; not to understand that no man can be dishonest, without soon being found out, and that when his lack of principle is discovered, nearly every avenue to success is closed against him forever. The public very properly shun all whose integrity is doubted. No matter how polite and pleasant and accommodating a man may be, none of us dare to deal with him if we suspect "false weights and measures." Strict honesty, not only lies at the foundation of all success in life (financially), but in every other respect.

Uncompromising integrity of character is invaluable. It secures to its possessor a peace and joy which cannot be attained without it—which no amount of money, or houses and lands can purchase. A man who is known to be strictly honest, may be ever so poor, but he has the purses of all the community at his disposal—for all know that if he promises to return what he borrows, he will never disappoint them. As a mere matter of selfishness, therefore, if a man had no higher motive for being honest, all will find that the maxim of Dr. Franklin can never fail to be true, that "honesty is the best policy."

To get rich, is not always equivalent to being successful. "*There are many rich poor men,*" while there are many others, honest and devout men and women, who have never possessed so much money as some rich persons squander in a week, but who are nevertheless really richer and happier than any man can ever be while he is a transgressor of the higher laws of his being.

The inordinate love of money, no doubt, may be and is "the root of all evil," but money itself, when properly used, is not only a "handy thing to have in the house," but affords the gratification of blessing our race by enabling its possessor to enlarge the scope of human happiness and human influence. The desire for wealth is nearly universal, and none can say it is not laudable, provided the possessor of it accepts its responsibilities, and uses it as a friend to humanity.

Those who really desire to attain independence, have only to set their minds upon it, and adopt the proper means, as they do in regard to any other object which they wish to accomplish, and the thing is easily done.
as plain as the road to the mill."

simply in expending less than we earn; that seems to be a very simple problem. Mr. Micawber, one of those happy creations of the genial Dickens, puts the case in a strong light when he says that to have annual income of twenty pounds per annum, and spend twenty pounds and sixpence, is to be the most miserable of men; whereas, to have an income of only twenty pounds, and spend but nineteen pounds and sixpence is to be the happiest of mortals. Many of my readers may say, "

Conclusion

The history of acquiring wealth, which is commerce, is a history of civilization, and wherever trade has flourished most, there, too, have art and science produced the noblest fruits. In fact, as a general thing, money-getters are the benefactors of our race. To them, in a great measure, are we indebted for our institutions of learning and of art, our academies, colleges and churches. It is no argument against the desire for, or the possession of wealth, to say that there are sometimes misers who hoard money only for the sake of hoarding and who have no higher aspiration than to grasp everything which comes within their reach. As we have sometimes hypocrites in religion, and demagogues in politics, so there are occasionally misers among, money-getters. These, however, are only exceptions to the general rule. But when, in this country, we find such a nuisance and stumbling block as a miser, we remember with gratitude that in America we have no laws of primogeniture, and that in the due course of nature the time will come when the hoarded dust will be scattered for the benefit of mankind.

<u>To all men and women</u>: make money honestly, and not otherwise, for Shakespeare has truly said, "*He that wants money, means, and content, is without three good friends.*"

Printed by Libri Plureos GmbH in Hamburg,
Germany